Recipes for Kids Cook Real Food

Companion recipe book for:

Kids Cook Real Food:
Cooking Class Curriculum

by Katie Kimball

www.KidsCookRealFood.com

This recipe book is an accompaniment to
Kids Cook Real Food: Cooking Class Curriculum.

Visit *www.kidscookrealfood.com/get-paperback-books* for ordering information or email *support@kidscookrealfood.com*.

Published in the United States by Kitchen Stewardship, LLC
www.KitchenStewardship.com

For use with *Kids Cook Real Food: Cooking Class Curriculum*

Ordering Information:
Contact the publisher at mailadmin@KitchenStewardship.com or visit www.KidsCookRealFood.com

Cover design by Mary Voogt.
Cover photos by Katie Kimball.

Publisher's Cataloging-in-Publication data
Kimball, Katie
Recipes for Kids Cook Real Food / Katie Kimball
56 p. ; cm.
ISBN: 978-1-947031-79-1
1. CKB120000 COOKING / Cooking with Kids I. Kimball, Katie II. Recipes for Kids Cook Real Food
LCCN: 2017906060

Second Edition

Table of Contents

Ants On A Log

SERVINGS VARY *BEGINNER 1*

Ingredients

- celery ribs
- peanut butter, or other nut butter
- raisins

(No specific amounts are given for this recipe, especially since it will most likely be Beginners who are making it and they'll be practicing their spreading skills.)

Instructions

1. Wash the celery ribs, removing any unwanted parts.
2. Cut the celery into 3 - 5 inch length logs.
3. Use a dull knife to spread the peanut butter over the celery logs.
4. Place raisins on the log, making an ant trail.
5. Ants On A Log can be kept as a snack for a few days when stored in the fridge.

Basic Rice

SERVINGS VARY *INTERMEDIATE 5*

Type of Rice	How Much Rice?	How Much Water?	Cooking Time
Basic White (long grain)	1 cup *or 195 grams*	2 cups *or 480 mL*	15 - 18 minutes
Basic Brown (long grain)	1 cup *or 195 grams*	2 cups *or 480 mL*	40 - 45 minutes
Basmati & Jasmine	1 cup *or 195 grams*	1 1/2 cups *or 360 mL*	15 - 25 minutes

You really should check *your* rice package for the ratio of rice to water. It will range from {1 cup rice per 1 cup water} to {1 cup rice per 3 cups water}.

Some folks rinse rice in a strainer before cooking. This can yield a better result (less sticky/starchy) but is not 100% necessary in my opinion.

For troubleshooting information, check out the Challenges You May Encounter section at the end of Intermediate Class 5.

Instructions

1. Measure rice and water into pot with a lid. Usually it is 1 cup rice per every 2 cups water.
2. Give a gentle stir.
3. Turn the heat to high and bring to a boil, with the lid on.
4. Once the water is boiling, turn the heat to low. (If you have an electric stovetop, you may need to move the pot to a new burner.)
5. Keep the lid on the pot. NO PEEKING!
6. Set the timer (see the chart above).
7. The rice is done when you see little craters show up on the top surface. Let the rice sit — off the heat — for 5 minutes with the lid on for best fluff.

Best Gluten-Free Pumpkin Muffins Ever

MAKES 12+ *INTERMEDIATE 4, ADVANCED 4*

Ingredients

- 1 2/3 c. (one and two-thirds cup) gluten-free flour blend [recipe page 36] *200 grams*
- 1/2 tsp. (one-half teaspoon) cinnamon *2.5 mL*
- 1/2 tsp. (one-half teaspoon) nutmeg *2.5 mL*
- 1/2 tsp. (one-half teaspoon) cloves *2.5 mL*
- 1/4 tsp. (one-fourth teaspoon) baking powder *1.2 mL*
- 1 tsp. (one teaspoon) baking soda *5 mL*
- 3/4 tsp. (three-fourths teaspoon) salt *3.7 mL*
- 1 c. (one cup) sucanat *200 grams* or 3/4 c. (three-fourths cup) honey *255 grams*
- 1/2 c. (one-half cup) butter *120 grams* or coconut oil *50 grams*, melted
- 1/4 c. (one-fourth cup) cold water *60 mL*
- 1 1/4 c. (one and one-fourth cup) pumpkin *280 grams*
- 2 eggs

Instructions

1. Mix the dry ingredients together: flour, cinnamon, nutmeg, cloves, baking powder, baking soda, and salt.
2. Add all the rest of the ingredients right on top. Note: the coconut oil will solidify when it touches the cold eggs, so be ready to stir. Add the eggs last.
3. Stir or beat well.
4. Preheat the oven to 325° F *(165° C)*.
5. Line muffin tin with paper muffin cups and pour about 3/4 (three-quarters) full into 12 muffin cups, filling evenly.
6. Bake for 40 - 45 minutes (20 - 25 for 24 mini muffins).
7. You might have a little left over, and a mini loaf pan is usually just right for the extra.

Best Honey Whole Wheat Pumpkin Muffins Ever

MAKES 12+ *INTERMEDIATE 4, ADVANCED 4*

Ingredients

- 1 2/3 c. (one and two-thirds cup) whole wheat flour *200 grams*
- 1/2 tsp. (one-half teaspoon) cinnamon *2.5 mL*
- 1/2 tsp. (one-half teaspoon) nutmeg *2.5 mL*
- 1/2 tsp. (one-half teaspoon) cloves *2.5 mL*
- 1/4 tsp. (one-fourth teaspoon) baking powder *1.2 mL*
- 1 tsp. (one teaspoon) baking soda *5 mL*
- 3/4 tsp. (three-fourths teaspoon) salt *3.7 mL*
- 3/4 c. (three-fourths cup) honey *255 grams* or 1 c. (one cup) sucanat *200 grams*
- 1/2 c. (one-half cup) butter *120 grams* or coconut oil *50 grams*, melted
- 1/4 c. (one-fourth cup) cold water *60 mL*
- 1 c. (one cup) pumpkin *280 grams*
- 2 eggs

Instructions

1. Mix the dry ingredients together: flour, cinnamon, nutmeg, cloves, baking powder, baking soda, and salt.
2. Add all the rest of the ingredients right on top. Note: the coconut oil will solidify when it touches the cold eggs, so be ready to stir. Add the eggs last.
3. Stir or beat well and preheat the oven to 325° F *(165° C)*.
4. Line muffin tin with paper muffin cups and pour about 3/4 (three-quarters) full into 12 muffin cups, filling evenly.
5. Bake for 40 - 45 minutes at 325° F *(165° C)* (20 - 25 for 24 mini muffins).
6. You might have a little left over, and a mini loaf pan is usually just right for the extra. *For photos and more go to* www.KidsCookRealFood.com/recipes *and see the Class 4, Intermediate section.*

Chickpea Wraps

SERVES 4 *ADVANCED 7*

Ingredients

- 1 c. (one cup) carrot, finely chopped or shredded *110 grams*
- 1 1/2 c. (one and one-half cup) onions, diced *225 grams*
- 3 cloves garlic, minced
- 1 tsp. (one teaspoon) ground cumin *5 mL*
- 1/4 c. (one-fourth cup) parsley, minced *6 grams*
  OR 1 Tbs. (one tablespoon) dried parsley *15 mL*
- 1 3/4 c. (one and three-fourths cup) chickpeas, cooked and drained *[about 1 can, also called garbanzo beans]* *290 grams*
- 1 1/2 Tbs. (one and one-half tablespoon) tahini or peanut butter, *optional* *22.5 mL*
- 1/3 c. (one-third cup) flour, any kind *40 grams*
- 1/2 tsp. (one-half teaspoon) baking soda *2.5 mL*
- 1 tsp. (one teaspoon) salt *5 mL*
- 4 Tbs. (four tablespoons) fat for cooking: *olive oil, coconut oil, lard, butter, etc.* *60 mL*

Instructions

1. If using a food processor, shred cheese first and remove before starting the recipe. Saves on dishes!
2. Shred the carrots to fill one cup.
3. Change to the blade and mince the garlic in the food processor. Remove to a small plate to hold for a while.
4. Pulse the onions just enough to get them chopped. Sauté with the carrots in 2 tablespoons fat for about 5 - 10 minutes over medium heat, stirring occasionally. A lid will move things along faster.
5. Add the cumin and garlic to the pan at the last minute.
6. *Note: If using fresh parsley, process it before the chickpeas.*
7. Process the cooked chickpeas into a paste (it will be pretty dry).

8. Add the sautéed vegetables to the food processor and process for a few seconds until everything is mixed together.
9. Mix in the peanut butter/tahini and dried parsley.
10. Combine the flour, baking soda, and salt in a small bowl, then mix into chickpeas.
11. Fry small, thin patties in melted fat over medium-low heat for 1 - 2 minutes, until just beginning to brown.
12. Turn over and fry the other side until browned and crispy, but don't worry too much about the perfect cook time. They only need to be warmed as there's no raw meat or egg for safety considerations.
13. Serve in warm tortillas. Our favorite toppings include lettuce, homemade ranch dressing, yellow mustard, sliced red onion, thinly sliced cucumbers, and of course, shredded cheese.

Notes

- No food processor? You can use a hand blender or even a potato masher to smash the chickpeas and simply stir in the remaining ingredients. Be sure to finely chop the onions and shred or very finely chop the carrots if you don't have a tool to blend them into the mixture.

- This recipe freezes fine, by the way. Freeze it in the "mush" form and then fry up patties when you're ready to eat.

Easy Gluten-Free Corn Bread

MAKES 9 SQUARES *BEGINNER 8*

Ingredients

- 2 c. (two cups) whole cornmeal *320 grams*
- 1 tsp. (one teaspoon) salt *5 mL*
- 3 tsp. (three teaspoons) baking powder *15 mL*
- 1 1/4 c. (one and one-fourth cup) milk *300 mL*
- 2 eggs
- 1/4 c. (one-fourth cup) butter, melted *[see directions]* *60 grams*
- 1 - 2 Tbs. (one to two tablespoons) honey or maple syrup *15-30 mL*

Instructions

1. Preheat the oven to 400° F *(200° C)*.
2. While the oven is warming up, put the butter in an 8x8-inch glass dish (or a 8 or 9-inch round pan) in the oven to melt the butter. This saves you a dish to clean up!
3. Whisk the cornmeal, salt, and baking powder together. Make a well and add the milk, eggs, butter, and sweetener. Whisk together thoroughly.
4. Bake at 400° F *(200° C)* for 20 - 25 minutes, until a knife inserted in the center comes out clean and you can feel that it's done. (Stick the knife near the edge, then near the center. They should feel the same — or almost the same. You can tell if the center is still mushy either with the knife or by tapping with your finger.)
5. Serve warm.
6. Store leftovers on the counter for 2 - 3 days or in the refrigerator for longer.

Easy Whole Wheat Happy Rolls

MAKES 24 *BEGINNER 8*

If you have a bread machine:

Ingredients

- 1 1/2 c. (one and one-half cup) water and whey *360 mL*
- 1/3 c. (one-third cup) olive oil *80 mL*
- 1/4 c. (one-fourth cup) honey *85 grams*
- 4 1/2 c. (four and one-half cups) whole wheat flour *540 grams*
- 1 egg
- 2 tsp. (two teaspoons) salt *10 mL*
- 1 Tbs. (one tablespoon) yeast *15 mL*

Instructions

1. In a bread machine, stir together the water, whey, oil, honey and flour.
2. Leave on the counter (or in the bread machine – unplugged) to soak overnight.
3. The next day, add the egg, salt and yeast.
4. Turn the bread machine on the dough cycle, which should take about 2 hours. *(No machine? No problem. See further instructions at* www.KidsCookRealFood.com/recipes *in the Class 8, Beginner section. There's more info there about the use of whey, as well.)*
5. Make balls about the size of a Clementine orange. Use plenty of flour to keep things from sticking. You'll have about 24 balls.
6. Cover with a light towel. Allow the dough to rise in the warmest spot you can find for 45 minutes.
7. Preheat the oven to 375° F *(190° C)*.
8. Bake rolls for 15 - 20 minutes. When they're done, they will sound hollow when you tap on them.

The No-soak Instructions:

Simply skip Steps 1 - 3 above (don't bother with the whey) and put all the ingredients into the bread machine, liquids first (water, oil, honey and egg) and then the flour and yeast.

No Bread Machine:

If you don't have a bread machine (or even if you do but want a super easy recipe for your littles) this recipe from my friend Laura of HeavenlyHomemakers.com is kind of amazing. She makes it bigger for sandwiches, smaller for speed, and has all sorts of tips. You can even use the recipe for fresh rolls out of the freezer. Laura was so kind, she even let us share her recipe with you. More details and a link to her recipe tips at www.KidsCookRealFood.com/recipes.

Stir-and-Pour Version:

Ingredients

- 4 c. (four cups) whole wheat flour *480 grams*
- 2 tsp. (two teaspoons) active rise yeast *10 mL*
- 2 Tbsp. (two tablespoons) sucanat or sugar or honey *30 mL*
- 1 tsp. (one teaspoon) sea salt *5 mL*
- 1 egg, optional
- ¼ cup (one-fourth cup) heavy cream, *optional 60 mL*
- 2 c. (two cups) warm water *480 mL*

Instructions

1. Stir all ingredients together.
2. Cover and allow to sit for 30 minutes.
3. Pour contents into buttered muffin tins or silicone muffin cups.
4. Bake at 350° F *(180° C)* for 20 - 25 minutes or until lightly browned.
5. Serve right away.

Recipe used with permission. Author: Laura of HeavenlyHomemakers.com

Egg Fried Rice

SERVES 2 *INTERMEDIATE 3, ADVANCED 3*

Ingredients

- 1 Tbs. (one tablespoon) sesame or olive oil *15 mL*
- 1/2 c. (one-half cup) diced red pepper, *optional 90 grams*
- 1 Tbs. (one tablespoon) rice vinegar, *optional 15 mL*
- 1 - 2 cloves garlic
- 2 c. (two cups) cooked rice *380 grams*
- 1/4 tsp. (one-fourth teaspoon) turmeric *1.2 mL*
- 1/4 tsp. (one-fourth teaspoon) powdered ginger *1.2 mL*
- 1/2 tsp. (one-half teaspoon) salt *2.5 mL*
- 1/8 tsp. (one-eighth teaspoon) black pepper *.6 mL*
- 1 Tbs. (one tablespoon) oil — *again 15 mL*
- 2 - 4 eggs

Instructions

1. Press the garlic and set aside to maximize health benefits.
2. Heat the oil over medium heat in a pot or deep pan large enough to fit everything (or a wok, if you've got one).
3. Add the diced peppers *(optional)*.
4. Sauté until limp/cooked.
5. Add the garlic and vinegar *(optional)* and sauté for one minute.
6. Add rice and seasonings and cook over low to medium low heat, stirring often, until everything is heated through.
7. Push the rice aside and make a spot where you can see the bottom of the pot. Turn the heat up.
8. Add another tablespoon of oil. When it's hot pour in the eggs.
9. Whisk them in the hole until they're partly cooked, then stir them all around in the rice.

Notes

- You can make this with or without eggs, actually. Add other veggies like frozen peas, corn, green beans or broccoli right in the rice – it makes a great side dish.
- Technically fried rice is supposed to be made only with already cooled rice. It tasted great our way, but if you want to make it "for real" there are some links to great recipes at *www.KidsCookRealFood.com/recipes*
- Made too much fried rice? Place extra fried rice into a container or bag and freeze. *(If using a bag, be sure to lay flat on a cookie tray.)* Don't forget to label and date your food! Simply thaw and reheat on the stove top with a little bit of water to help moisten the fried rice.

Everything Eggs: Boiled

SERVINGS VARY *INTERMEDIATE 3, ADVANCED 6*

Ingredients

- eggs
- salt
- ice cubes

Instructions

1. Place the eggs in a pot that has a lid. Place the lid next to the stove.
2. Cover the eggs with cold water.
3. Add generous dash of salt, 1/4 to 1/2 teaspoon *(1.2 - 2.5 mL).*
4. Turn the burner to high and bring the water to a boil with the lid on.
5. When the water boils, turn the heat off (move the pot off the burner if on an electric stove). Leave the lid on.
6. Set a timer for 12 minutes. (12 = a dozen eggs, so it's easy to remember!)
7. While the timer ticks, prepare a big bowl of ice cubes and water.
8. When the timer beeps, remove the eggs one at a time with a slotted spoon or tongs and submerge in ice water until no longer warm.
9. Hard-boiled eggs are easiest to peel if you do it right away, OR use a pencil to mark the eggs with an X (or whatever mark you decide) so when you put them in your fridge, you'll know which ones are boiled and which ones aren't.
10. Hard boiled eggs last up to one week in the fridge.

Everything Eggs: Fried

SERVINGS VARY *INTERMEDIATE 3, ADVANCED 6*

Ingredients

- eggs
- butter or coconut oil
- salt, pepper

Instructions

1. Preheat your cooking surface and turn the heat to medium-low.
2. Sizzle test! (Flick some water in the pan. If it "dances" or sizzles, the pan is hot enough.)
3. Add cooking fat.
4. Crack an egg into a small bowl to check for shells. Gently slide the egg onto the hot surface.
5. If making hard-fried eggs, you can break the yolk at any time.
6. When the edges are very white and solid, use a thin, rigid spatula to scrape quickly under the egg and flip. If you're trying for a soft-fried egg, be gentle!
7. Allow the second side to cook. For a soft-fried egg, wait until the white part is just cooked when you peek underneath. For a hard-fried egg, you can cook longer.
8. Add salt and pepper to taste at any time during the cooking process or tell your eaters to add it at the table.

Notes

- A hard-fried egg has a completely cooked and solid yolk. Sometimes this is referred to as "over-hard."

- A soft-fried egg has a runny yolk. Sometimes this referred to as "sunny-side-up" or "over-easy."

Everything Eggs: Scrambled

SERVINGS VARY *INTERMEDIATE 3, ADVANCED 6*

Ingredients

- butter
- eggs
- cottage cheese or sour cream or milk
- salt, pepper

Instructions

1. Preheat a pan on medium heat. Place some butter (or other cooking fat) in the pan. If you're adding any meat or veggies, sauté them first before the eggs.
2. Crack the eggs into a medium bowl and whisk until uniform.
3. If adding cottage cheese or sour cream, the ratio is 2 - 3 tablespoons *(30-45 mL)* of dairy for every two eggs.
4. Add eggs to the pan. Cook low and slow.
5. Let the bottom of the eggs cook before you stir. While you're waiting, add salt and pepper to taste (or let people know they're unseasoned eggs).
6. Use a lawnmower stir (a term we teach in the Foundations 101 class on stirring in *Kids Cook Real Food*) to scrape the bottom back and forth, pushing the runny parts to the middle.
7. To add cheese, do it just before eggs are cooked.

Notes

- Don't leave your eggs in the pan because they will continue to cook even though the heat is off and can become overcooked.
- Great add-ins for scrambled eggs: bulk or sliced sausage, bacon, spinach or other greens, peppers, onions, cooked potatoes, mushrooms, or other veggies to your liking.
- Omelets are a little different. Learn how at *www.KidsCookRealFood.com/recipes*

Favorite Gluten-Free Pancakes

MAKES 4-5 DOZEN *INTERMEDIATE 6*

Ingredients

- 3 c. (three cups) gluten-free flour blend *[recipe page 36]* *360 grams*
- 1 1/4 c. (one and one-fourth cup) whole milk or yogurt *300 mL*
- 1 1/4 c. (one and one-fourth cup) water *300 mL*
- 1/4 c. (one-fourth cup) apple cider vinegar *60 mL*
- 1/4 c. (one-fourth cup) coconut oil, melted *25 grams*
- 4 eggs
- 3 tsp. (three teaspoons) baking powder *15 mL*
- 1 tsp. (one teaspoon) baking soda *5 mL*
- 1 tsp. (one teaspoon) salt *5 mL*

Instructions

1. The night before: Mix flour, milk or yogurt, water, and vinegar. Leave batter on the counter overnight to soak (up to 24 hours).
2. In the morning: Mix in the eggs and coconut oil. (If your coconut oil is solid, it can be handy to melt it in the pan you cook your pancakes in or a metal measuring cup on a griddle.)
3. Sprinkle baking powder, soda, and salt evenly over the top and mix in thoroughly. There should be some bubbling from the interaction of the vinegar and baking soda.
4. Heat a griddle or frying pan over medium heat. Add fat for cooking. Pour 2 or 3-inch circles of batter.
5. Flip each pancake when the edges look dry and bubbles pop on the top of the pancake batter. They only need 5-15 seconds to cook the second side.

Note

- You can make this recipe without soaking by mixing everything up at once.

Favorite Whole Wheat Pancakes

MAKES 4-5 DOZEN *INTERMEDIATE 6*

Ingredients

- 3 c. (three cups) whole wheat flour *360 grams*
- 1 c. (one cup) milk or yogurt *240 mL*
- 1 c. (one cup) water *240 mL*
- 1/4 c. (one-fourth cup) apple cider vinegar *60 mL*
- 1/4 c. (one-fourth cup) coconut oil, melted *25 mL*
- 4 eggs
- 3 tsp. (three teaspoons) baking powder *15 mL*
- 1 tsp. (one teaspoon) baking soda *5 mL*
- 1 tsp. (one teaspoon) salt *5 mL*

Instructions

1. The night before: Mix flour, milk or yogurt, water, and vinegar. Leave batter on the counter overnight to soak (up to 24 hours).
2. In the morning: Mix in the eggs and coconut oil. (If your coconut oil is solid, it can be handy to melt it in the pan you cook your pancakes in or a metal measuring cup on a griddle.)
3. Sprinkle baking powder, soda, and salt evenly over the top and mix in thoroughly. There should be some bubbling from the interaction of the vinegar and baking soda.
4. Heat a griddle or frying pan over medium heat. Add fat for cooking. Pour 2 or 3-inch circles of batter.
5. Flip each pancake when the edges look dry and bubbles pop on the top of the pancake batter. They only need 5-15 seconds to cook the second side.

Note

- You can make this recipe without soaking by mixing everything up at once.

Grain-Free Coconut Flour Blueberry Pancakes

MAKES ABOUT 16-18 *INTERMEDIATE 6*

Ingredients

- 4 eggs
- 1/4 c. (one-fourth cup) unsweetened applesauce *60 grams*
- 1/4 c. (one-fourth cup) coconut milk or whole milk *60 mL*
- 1/2 (one-half) banana, mashed, *optional*
- 1/4 tsp. (one-fourth teaspoon) salt *1.2 mL*
- 1/2 tsp. (one-half teaspoon) nutmeg *2.5 mL*
- 1/4 tsp. (one-fourth teaspoon) baking soda *1.2 mL*
- 1 tsp. (one teaspoon) apple cider vinegar *5 mL*
- 1/4 c. (one-fourth cup) coconut oil, melted *25 grams*
- 3 - 4 Tbs. (three to four tablespoons) coconut flour *45-60 mL*
- 1/2 - 3/4 c. (one-half to three-fourths cup) blueberries *75-110 grams*

Instructions

1. *Prep note:* If your coconut oil is solid, melt it. I use my metal measuring cup right on my griddle as it preheats so I don't dirty another pot!
2. In a medium-sized bowl, mix all the ingredients except the coconut oil, coconut flour and blueberries. *(I like to use a tool that can mash my banana right in the bowl.)*
3. Heat a griddle or large pan over medium heat.
4. Whisk in the melted coconut oil quickly - it tends to solidify when it hangs out with cold eggs too long.
5. Add the coconut flour, starting with 3 tablespoons. Watch for clumps.
6. Whisk thoroughly until uniform.
7. Grease your cooking surface with ample fat (coconut oil, tallow or lard are great choices).

8. Ladle out 3-inch pancakes, adding blueberries right into each pancake.
9. Over medium-low or medium heat, cook a minute or so, until bubbles form on top, then flip and cook another 30 seconds or so until brown on the bottom.

Notes

- If your blueberries are too fat and interfere with browning the second side, just serve them at the table to put on top of the cooked pancakes. Huckleberries are perfect to go inside the pancakes.

Grain-Free Pumpkin Pancakes

MAKES ABOUT 30 *INTERMEDIATE 6*

Ingredients

- 9 eggs
- 2 c. (two cups) canned pumpkin *560 grams*
- 1 tsp. (one teaspoon) cinnamon *5 mL*
- 1/4 tsp. (one-fourth teaspoon) cloves *1.2 mL*
- 1/2 tsp. (one-half teaspoon) ginger *2.5 mL*
- 1/2 tsp. (one-half teaspoon) nutmeg *2.5 mL*
- 1 tsp. (one teaspoon) salt *5 mL*
- 1/2 tsp. (one-half teaspoon) baking soda *2.5 mL*
- 1 - 2 Tbs. (one or two tablespoons) maple syrup *15-30 mL*
- 2 tsp. (two teaspoons) vanilla *10 mL*
- 3 Tbs. (three tablespoons) packed coconut flour *45 mL*

Instructions

1. Crack all the eggs into a large bowl.
2. Add pumpkin.
3. Whisk together until uniform.
4. Sprinkle the spices over the top: cinnamon, cloves, ginger, and nutmeg.
5. Add the salt, baking soda, maple syrup and vanilla.
6. Stir well until uniform again.
7. Get any clumps out of the coconut flour. Sprinkle it over the top and then stir well.
8. Preheat your pan to medium heat and add a good bit of cooking fat.
9. Pour small circles to make it easy to flip.
10. Flip when the edges look dry (it takes about a minute).

Homemade Chicken Rice-a-Roni Substitute

SERVES 2-4 *ADVANCED 7*

Ingredients

- 1 Tbs. (one tablespoon) butter or olive oil *15 mL*
- 1 c. (one cup) brown rice, uncooked *195 grams*
- 2 c. (two cups) chicken broth [1 can plus a little water = 2 cups] *475 mL*
- 1 onion, diced
- 1 - 2 celery ribs, diced
- 1/2 tsp. (one-half teaspoon) salt *2.5 mL*
- 1/8 tsp. (one-eighth teaspoon) pepper *.6 mL*

Instructions

1. Sauté onion and celery in butter or oil about 5 minutes until onions are glossy and the celery is limp.
2. Add uncooked rice and stir around over medium heat or higher for a few minutes, until you just start to see some of the rice turn brown (toasted).
3. Pour chicken broth in CAREFULLY and add salt and pepper.
4. Bring to a boil.
5. Reduce heat, cover, and simmer on very low heat for 15 minutes for white rice or 45 minutes for brown (or follow your package instructions). No peeking!

Notes

- You can make this into a heartier "beans and rice" side dish by adding one can (or 2 cups cooked) beans and stirring until heated through. Try chickpeas, black, or kidney beans.

Homemade Finger Gelatin or "Gellies"

MAKES 9-12 *BEGINNER 6*

Ingredients

- 3 c. (three cups) fruit juice, divided into 2 cups and 1 cup *720 mL*
- 6 Tbs. (six tablespoons) gelatin *90 mL*

Adults, see *www.kitchenstewardship.com/kcrfresources* for where to source gelatin.

Instructions

1. Measure 2 cups *(480 mL)* juice into a small pot.
2. Heat gently over medium (adult or older kid job).
3. Measure 1 cup *(240 mL)* cold juice into a 4-cup or larger bowl.
4. Sprinkle gelatin over the cold juice and whisk thoroughly.
5. When the juice on the stove is just steaming a little and hot/painful to touch, not boiling, turn off the heat.
6. Pour the heated juice into the cold juice and whisk thoroughly (adult or older kid job).
7. Pour it all into a glass baking dish to the desired height (8x8-inch or oval casserole dishes works great).
8. Chill at least 4 hours in the refrigerator. When firm, cut into squares with a butter knife or use cookie cutters to make shapes.
9. Store in the refrigerator up to one week. These can be shelf stable long enough for lunch or snack, but not for days.

Notes

- Want to know how to make "gellies" or "gummies" with whole fruit? *Visit www.KidsCookRealFood.com/recipes*

Homemade Gelatin Cups

SERVES 4-8 *BEGINNER 6*

Ingredients

- 4 c. (four cups) fruit juice, divided into 3 cups and 1 cup *960 mL*
- 2 Tbs. (two tablespoons) gelatin *30 mL*

Adults, see *www.kitchenstewardship.com/kcrfresources* for where to source gelatin.

Instructions

1. If you have a 4-cup measuring cup with a lid, you can use that to make the gelatin. Otherwise, you'll need any container that can hold 4 cups.
2. Measure 3 cups *(720 mL)* of fruit juice and pour it into a medium pot.
3. Turn the stove on to medium heat (adult or older kid job).
4. Measure 1 cup *(240 mL)* of fruit juice. Pour into large bowl.
5. Whisk the gelatin into 1 cup *(240 mL)* of juice until it is uniform (a term we teach in the Foundations 101 class on stirring in *Kids Cook Real Food*).
6. When you see steam rising off the juice warming on the stove, it's hot enough. You don't have to boil it.
7. Pour the hot juice into the cold gelatin/juice mixture (adult job or guided job).
8. Whisk thoroughly (but slowly so you don't splash hot juice). This might be an adult job, guided job or kid job depending on maturity of the child.
9. You can leave the gelatin in one big bowl or pour it into individual bowls at this point.
10. Chill in the refrigerator for at least 4 hours and eat cold with a spoon.
11. Store in the refrigerator up to one week.

Homemade Gluten-Free Crackers

MAKES 5-6 DOZEN *INTERMEDIATE 7*

Ingredients

- 1 1/4 c. (one and one-fourth cup) gluten-free flour blend [recipe page 36 or see recipe notes] *150 mL*
- 1 1/2 Tbs. (one and one-half tablespoons) honey or sucanat *22.5 mL*
- 1/2 tsp. (one-half teaspoon) salt *2.5 mL*
- 1/4 tsp. (one-fourth teaspoon) paprika *1.2 mL*
- 4 Tbs. (four tablespoons) cold butter or solid coconut oil *60 mL*
- 1/4 c. (one-fourth cup) water *60 mL*
- 1/4 tsp. (one-fourth teaspoon) vanilla *1.2 mL*
- salt for topping

Instructions

1. Combine the flour, sucanat (if using), salt and paprika in a medium bowl.
2. Using a pastry blender or two butter knives, cut the fat thoroughly into the dry mixture until it looks like large crumbs, no bigger than a pea.
3. Combine the water, vanilla, and honey (if using). Add slowly to the flour mixture, watching for all the flour to be incorporated.
4. Mix well until combined, but only until the dough comes together to assure the most tender crackers.
5. Preheat the oven to 400° F *(200° C)*.
6. Line a cookie sheet with parchment paper and roll out one-fourth to one-half of the dough, as thinly as possible without tearing. *(By rolling on your cookie sheet, you don't have to worry about transferring the dough.)*
7. Use a pizza cutter or sharp knife and cut the dough into squares or triangles, about 1 1/2 inches each. Fork pokes make them look extra authentic.
8. Sprinkle the squares lightly with salt.

9. Repeat steps 6 - 8 with the remaining pieces of dough.
10. Bake the crackers, one sheet at a time, until crisp and browned: 5 to 10 minutes. (If you want to bake two trays at once, you can position your racks on the very top and bottom of the oven, and switch the trays halfway through the baking time.)
11. As the thinner crackers on the edges begin to brown, remove them and return the remaining crackers to the oven to finish baking. These crackers bake quickly, so watch them closely – 30 seconds can turn them from golden brown to toast!
12. Extra crispy: If you can catch them before they're turning brown, turn off the oven and leave the crackers in as it cools. Check them after 5, 10 and 15 minutes to make sure they're not browning too much.
13. Cool completely before storing in an airtight container.

Notes

- If you don't want to commit to a big batch of GF flour, use a heaping half cup each of sorghum flour, rice flour, buckwheat flour and 1/2 cup + 3 Tbs. arrowroot for a double batch.
- For extra stability if baking gluten-free – although none of our testers had trouble with crumbly dough or crackers – you could add 1/4 teaspoon *(1.2 mL)* xanthan gum or powdered psyllium husk to the dry ingredients.
- Want to make crackers using wheat? Simply swap the GF blend for whole wheat flour and follow the recipe!

Homemade Mayonnaise

MAKES 1 CUP *BONUS CLASS*

Ingredients

- 1 egg, ideally from pastured chickens
- 1/2 tsp. (one-half teaspoon) mustard powder, *optional* *2.5 mL*
- 1 Tbs. (1 tablespoon) apple cider vinegar or lemon juice *15 mL*
- 1/2 tsp. (one-half teaspoon) salt *2.5 mL*
- 1 c. olive oil *235 mL*
- 1/4 tsp (one-fourth teaspoon) garlic powder, *optional* *1.2 mL*
- 1/4 tsp (one-fourth teaspoon) paprika, *optional* *1.2 mL*
- 1/4 tsp (one-fourth teaspoon) onion powder, *optional* *1.2 mL*

Instructions

1. In a jar that fits your immersion blender, put the egg, mustard powder, vinegar or lemon juice, salt, and optional seasoning. A wide mouth pint jar is the perfect size.
2. Add the olive oil and wait a few seconds, allowing the egg to settle on the bottom. There's no need to drizzle in the oil!
3. Settle the immersion blender at the bottom of the jar. Whiz the ingredients with your immersion blender. The mayo should emulsify — become solid — quickly.
4. If it doesn't work (or it does and then the emulsion "breaks"), you can still fix it. Pour everything into a new container. Start over with a new egg + more lemon juice or vinegar. Mix that up and then pour the broken version in on top as if it is the oil in the original instructions.

Homemade Potato Salad

SERVES 4 *BONUS CLASS*

Ingredients

- 4 eggs
- 4 whole potatoes
- 4 dill pickle spears [fewer if they're big ol' whole pickles]
- 1 - 2 tsp. (one to two teaspoons) yellow mustard *5-10 mL*
- 1 Tbs. (one tablespoon) homemade mayo (recipe on previous page) *15 mL*
- 1/2 tsp. (one-half teaspoon) salt *2.5 mL*
- pepper to taste

Instructions

1. Hard boil the eggs. *See recipe page 14.*
2. Cool and peel them.
3. Dice into bite-sized cubes.
4. Peel the potatoes *(optional)*.
5. Dice potatoes into bite-sized cubes.
6. In a medium pot, cover the potatoes with water. Add some salt — about 1/8 -1/4 teaspoon *(.6 - 1.2 mL)*.
7. Cover and bring to a boil.
8. Turn heat to low and set a timer for 10 minutes.
9. Check the potatoes with a fork to see if they're soft all the way through. If not, wait 5 more minutes and check again.
10. Drain the water off the potatoes and allow them to cool.
11. Dice the pickles into tiny pieces with a sharp knife.
12. In a large bowl, combine the potatoes, eggs, pickles, mustard, and mayo.
13. Stir well using a Roller Coaster stir (a term we teach in the Foundations 101 class on stirring in Kids Cook Real Food). It will seem dry at first but keep going. If you're sure you have stirred thoroughly and it still seems dry, add more mustard and mayo.
14. For a fun zip, pour in a splash of pickle juice from the jar!

15. Add salt and pepper and stir well again.
16. Taste and see what you think!

Notes

- Many pickles have artificial colors in them (unfortunately) but it's getting easier to find brands that don't. Read the ingredients!
- This recipe is easy to double, triple or quadruple for families or parties.
- You can use any sort of cooked potatoes, even baked, if you want. The flavors will soak into the potatoes better if you mix it all up while they're slightly warm. But if the timing works better to cook the potatoes and eggs one day, refrigerate overnight and mix it up the next day, it will still taste good!

Homemade Salad Dressings

INTERMEDIATE 1

Italian Dressing

Ingredients

- 3/4 c. (three-fourths cup) extra virgin olive oil *175 mL*
- 1/4 - 1/2 c. (one-fourth to one-half cup) red or white wine vinegar *60-120 mL*
- 2 tsp. (two teaspoons) garlic powder *10 mL*
- 2 tsp. (two teaspoons) Italian seasoning *(see below for mix)* *10 mL*
- 1 tsp. (one teaspoon) salt *5 mL*
- 1/2 tsp. (one-half teaspoon) pepper *2.5 mL*
- 1 Tbs. (one tablespoon) Dijon mustard *15 mL*

Instructions

1. Mix the ingredients in order according to the list above.
2. You can mix it all right in a liquid measuring cup to make it easy to measure the oil, and then use a fork or small whisk to mix it all together. OR just mix/shake it in the container you're going to store the dressing in.
3. Store at room temperature for a month, preferably out of the light (use a solid container or store it in the cupboard).

If you don't have Italian seasoning, use:

- 1/2 tsp. (one-half teaspoon) dried basil *2.5 mL*
- 1/2 tsp. (one-half teaspoon) dried thyme *2.5 mL*
- 1/2 tsp. (one-half teaspoon) dried oregano *2.5 mL*
- 1/4 tsp. (one-fourth teaspoon) dried rosemary *1.2 mL*
- 1/4 tsp. (one-fourth teaspoon) dried marjoram *1.2 mL*

Ranch Dressing (without mix)

Ingredients

- 1 c. (one cup) of either: sour cream, yogurt, homemade mayo *245 grams*
- 1 Tbs. (one tablespoon) red wine vinegar *15 mL*
- 1/2 tsp. (one-half teaspoon) onion powder *2.5 mL*
- 1/4 tsp. (one-fourth teaspoon) garlic powder *1.2 mL*
- 1/4 tsp. (one-fourth teaspoon) dried parsley *1.2 mL*
- 1/4 tsp. (one-fourth teaspoon) dried dill *1.2 mL*
- 1/4 tsp. (one-fourth teaspoon) dried chives *1.2 mL*
- 1/4 tsp. (one-fourth teaspoon) salt *1.2 mL*
- 1/8 tsp. (one-eighth teaspoon) black pepper *.6 mL*
- A few shakes cayenne pepper, *optional*

Instructions

1. Mix ingredients together well until everything is uniform. For stronger flavor, double some or all of the dried herbs (parsley, dill, chives).
2. Store in the refrigerator and use as a dressing or veggie dip.

Ranch Dressing (with pre-made mix)

Ingredients

- 1 c. (one cup) of either: sour cream, yogurt, homemade mayo *245 grams*
- 1 tsp. - 1 Tbs. (one teaspoon to one tablespoon) red wine vinegar *5 - 15 mL*
- 2 tsp. (two teaspoons) ranch mix *10 mL* *[recipe included on page 33]*

Instructions

1. Mix ingredients together well until everything is uniform. Start with 1 teaspoon *(5 mL)* vinegar, taste it and see if you'd like it more tangy.
2. Thin with milk for pourable dressing.
3. Serve with raw veggies or salad.
4. Store in the refrigerator and use as a dressing or veggie dip.

5. The dip will last as long as the ingredients would have lasted on their own (often about two weeks after opening, for sour cream).

Note:

- The flavor will get a little stronger after a few hours as the herbs permeate the sour cream or other base. You can add 1/2 to 1 teaspoon *(2.5 - 5 mL)* more ranch mix if you'd like more flavor.

Homemade Seasoning Blends

BEGINNER 4

Taco Seasoning Mix

- 3 Tbs. (Dad) arrowroot or corn starch *45 mL*
- 2 Tbs. (Dad) chili powder *30 mL*
- 1 Tbs. (Dad) paprika *15 mL*
- 1 Tbs. (Dad) + 1 tsp. (Mom) + 1/2 tsp. (Kid) cumin *15 mL + 5 mL + 2.5 mL*
- 2 tsp. (Mom) + 1/2 tsp. (Kid) onion powder *10 + 2.5 mL*
- 2 tsp. (Mom) + 1/2 tsp. (Kid) garlic powder *10 + 2.5 mL*
- 1/4 tsp. (Baby) cayenne pepper, *optional* *1.2 mL*

To use: Mix 2 - 3 Tbs. *(30-45 mL)* mix with 1 pound *(500 grams)* cooked ground meat. (Two is pretty bland but for children might be just right; 3 is standard.) Pour in 3/4 - 1 cup *(180-240 mL)* water and bring to a boil. Reduce heat and stir over the heat until thickened. Add salt to taste (it makes a difference). 3 Tablespoons *(45 mL)* of Taco Seasoning Mix roughly equals one "packet" from the store if you are following a recipe that calls for packets.

Ranch Dressing Mix

- 2 Tbs. (Dad) dill *30 mL*
- 2 Tbs. (Dad) parsley *30 mL*
- 2 Tbs. (Dad) chives *30 mL*
- 4 Tbs. (Dad) onion powder *60 mL*
- 2 Tbs. (Dad) garlic powder *30 mL*
- 2 tsp. (Mom) black pepper *10 mL*
- 2 tsp. (Mom) salt *10 mL*
- 1/4 tsp. (Baby) cayenne pepper, *optional* *1.2 mL*

To use: See recipe on page 31 for ranch dressing.

St. Peter's Spicy Fish seasoning

- 2 Tbs. (Dad) garlic powder *30 mL*
- 2 Tbs. (Dad) salt *30 mL*
- 2 Tbs. (Dad) paprika *30 mL*
- 1 Tbs. (Dad) onion powder *15 mL*
- 1 Tbs. (Dad) black pepper *15 mL*
- 1 Tbs. (Dad) dried oregano *15 mL*
- 1 Tbs. (Dad) dried thyme *15 mL*
- 1 tsp. (Mom) + 1/2 tsp. (Kid) cayenne pepper *5 mL + 2.5 mL*

To Use: Sprinkle liberally on any fish and cook following instructions.

- Pan fry: Fry over medium in oil a few minutes (until edges turn white), then flip and fry until the fork test shows doneness.
- Bake: 350-400F° F *(180-200° C)* for about 10 minutes per inch of fish.
- Broil: 3-5 minutes, checking until done.

Guacamole

- 1 avocado
- 1 Tbs. (Dad) lime juice *15 mL*
- 1 tsp. (Mom) adobo seasoning (next page) *5 mL*
- 1/4 tsp. (Baby) salt *1.2 mL*

Instructions

1. Ask an adult to cut and pit the avocado.
2. Mash the avocado using one of these ways:
    a. Use a fork or large spoon and scrape out a little bit at a time into a small bowl (almost like you're scraping ice off a car or forming a shape on a sand castle bit by bit). It's easiest if you flip the utensil over, not the way you'd hold it to eat.
    b. Scoop into a bowl and mash with a fork or potato masher.
    c. Scoop all the avocado into a bowl with a spoon and use an immersion blender (hand blender) to whiz it up.
    d. Use a food processor.

3. Stir in the lime (or lemon), adobo seasoning and salt. You might start with less juice at first, since you can always add more but you can't take it out.
4. Taste and add more seasoning if you'd like.
5. Serve with chips and salsa, raw veggies (carrots, peppers, etc.) to dip, or with any Mexican meal.

Adobo Seasoning

- 1 Tbs. (Dad) + 1 tsp. (Mom) Mexican oregano *15 mL + 5 mL*
  [or 1 Tbs. (Dad) regular oregano *15 mL*]
- 1 Tbs. (Dad) cumin *15 mL*
- 1 Tbs. (Dad) garlic powder *15 mL*
- 1 Tbs. (Dad) onion powder *15 mL*
- 1 Tbs. (Dad) black pepper *15 mL*
- 1/4 tsp. (Baby) cayenne pepper *1.2 mL*

To Use: Sprinkle on chicken or use in Guacamole recipe.

Homemade Wonderful Gluten-Free Flour Blend

BEGINNER 4

Ingredients

- 2 c. (two cups) freshly ground buckwheat flour *240 grams*
- 2 c. (two cups) brown rice flour *290 grams*
- 2 c. (two cups) sorghum flour *270 grams*
- 2 1/2 c. (two and one-half cups) arrowroot powder *310 grams*

Instructions

1. In a large bowl, combine all ingredients and stir well.
2. Store in any airtight container, best kept in the freezer.
3. Use as directed in gluten-free recipes.

Mexican Rice

SERVES 2-4 *INTERMEDIATE 5*

Ingredients

- 1 c. (one cup) rice, white or brown *190 grams*
- 1 3/4 c. (one and three-fourths cups) water *420 mL*
- 1 c. (one cup) tomato sauce *[one 8-oz. little can]* *225 grams*
- 1 Tbs. (one tablespoon) taco seasoning *[recipe page 33]* *15 mL*
- 1/2 tsp. (one-half teaspoon) salt *5 mL*

Instructions

1. In a medium sized pot over medium heat, "toast" the rice. You don't need any fat (although you can add some if you want to). Stir the rice around and around constantly in the pot. After 2 - 7 minutes, it will start to get brown on the bottom. Keep stirring a LOT so you don't burn the rice.
2. After about half of it seems to be getting brown or "toasted," pour in the water *carefully*. It will start to sizzle and steam right away.
3. Turn the heat to high.
4. Add tomato sauce, taco seasoning, and salt. Stir well.
5. Bring to a boil, then turn down heat to low and put the lid on.
6. For white rice, cook 15 minutes. No Peeking! For brown rice, cook 45 minutes.
7. *Optional*: If you want "beans and rice" you can stir in a can of beans (black, pinto, kidney, etc.) after the rice is cooked. Leave on the heat (low) for a few minutes for the beans to get warm and stir them around well. You might need to add salt if the beans weren't salted already.

Oven Baked Apple Crisp

SERVES 4-6 *ADVANCED 4*

Ingredients

Base

- 5 - 10 small or 3 - 4 large apples
  [enough to fill a 9x13 baking dish about an inch deep]

Mix-ins

- 1/4 - 1/2 c. (one-fourth to one-half cup) sucanat or sugar *50-100 grams*
- 1/4 tsp. (one-fourth teaspoon) nutmeg *1.2 mL*
- 1/4 tsp. (one-fourth teaspoon) powdered ginger *1.2 mL*
- 1 tsp. (one teaspoon) cinnamon *5 mL*
- 3 Tbs. (three tablespoons) lemon juice *45 mL*
- 1/2 c. (one-half cup) raisins, *optional* *75 grams*
- 1/2 c. (one-half cup) chopped walnuts, *optional* *60 grams*

Topping

- 3/4 c. (three-fourths cup) rolled oats/oatmeal *30 grams*
- 1/3 c. (one-third cup) flour *[white, wheat, or GF blend]* *40 grams*
- Pinch of salt
- 1/2 c. (one-half cup) butter *120 grams*

Instructions

1. Grease a 9x13-inch baking dish.
2. Preheat the oven to 350° F *(180° C)*.
3. Slice your butter into medium thick (~1/2-inch) slices and set on a plate on the counter to get soft. *Don't skip this step!*
4. Wash apples. Quarter them (get the core out) and slice them thinly. Peeling is optional.
5. Cover the bottom of your dish at least an inch thick with apples, but deeper is fine.
6. In a medium bowl, combine the sucanat or sugar, nutmeg, ginger, and cinnamon. Divide the spice mixture in half.

7. Pour lemon juice and half the spice mixture over the apples. Use the Roller Coaster stir (a term we teach in the Foundations 101 class on stirring in Kids Cook Real Food) to fold it into all the apples.
8. If using nuts or raisins, add them to the apple mixture at this time.
9. In the bowl that still has half the spice mixture in it, add the oats, flour and salt. Stir well.
10. Using a pastry blender or two knives, cut the butter into that mixture. (If your butter is really soft, you can mash and stir it instead.)
11. Sprinkle the oat-butter mixture over the apples.
12. Bake at 350° F *(180° C)*. for 45 minutes OR 375° F *(190° C)* for 30 minutes. (If you're also baking something for dinner, that will determine which temperature to use.)
13. Poke with a fork to check doneness. The apples should be completely soft.
14. Serve warm if possible. Store leftovers in the refrigerator. Great re-warmed or cold!

Potato Hash

SERVINGS VARY *BEGINNER 3*

Basic Ingredients

- diced potatoes, *cooked or raw*
- salt, pepper, and garlic powder to taste

Optional Add-In Ingredients

- onions, diced
- bell peppers, diced
- mushrooms, diced
- zucchini, diced
- spinach or other greens
- herbs
- eggs, fried on the side or added to hash

Instructions

1. Heat a large pan and add a tablespoon or two of fat.
2. Add the cubed potatoes and stir to cover.
    - **If potatoes are raw:** cover and cook over medium-low heat, stirring every few minutes, for at least 10 minutes, until potatoes are getting soft. If using any other raw veggies like onions or peppers, add them with the raw potatoes.
    - **If potatoes are cooked:** start with very crispy raw veggies like onion or pepper first, and give them a 5 - 10 minute head start on the potatoes. Once you add the cooked potatoes, follow step 3, but the heat can be up at medium and it won't take very long. You want to watch for a little browning or crisping on the potatoes and feel that they're warmed up.
3. Once the potatoes are cooked and heated through, add mushrooms or zucchini.

4. Add herbs or seasoning as you like, including a heavy sprinkle of salt. (Italian herb blends or herbs de Provence are easy to use in a hash, or just parsley and garlic powder.)
5. Stir the vegetables around, scraping the bottom. Move food from the bottom to top and inside to out. When everything is soft enough to eat and it smells fragrant, you're ready to serve!

Notes

- To add eggs, you can either add a bit of fat after the veggies are cooked, crack a few eggs right into the hash, and mix them around until cooked to make a scramble. Or just make soft-fried eggs in another skillet and serve them on top of the potato hash.

- For a fun twist, add shredded cheese as a garnish on top.

- Some call this "American Fries" or fried potatoes.

Refried Beans

MAKES 2+ CANS WORTH *ADVANCED 5*

Ingredients

- 2 Tbs. (two tablespoons) olive oil, lard, or coconut oil *30 mL*
- 1 c. (one cup) onions, chopped *150 grams*
- 1 tsp. (one teaspoon) ground cumin *5 mL*
- 1/2 tsp. (one-half teaspoon) dried Mexican oregano *2.5 mL* [use regular oregano if you don't have Mexican]
- 1/2 - 1 tsp. (one-half to one teaspoon) salt *2.5 - .5 mL*
- 2 - 3 large cloves garlic, minced
- 3 1/2 c. (three and one-half cups) cooked pinto, kidney or black beans *560 grams*
- 1/2 c. (one-half cup) cheddar cheese, grated, *optional* *60 grams* [for extra zing, use jalapeño jack cheese]

Instructions

1. **If soaking dry beans:** start with 1 1/2 cups before soaking (or cook extra and freeze).
2. Refer to the advanced section of class 5 for cooking instructions.
3. Drain cooked beans and keep some of the cooking liquid to thin the refried beans.
4. In the pot from the cooked beans, heat the oil. Add the onions and cook over medium heat, stirring occasionally, until the onions are translucent (about 5-10 minutes).
5. Add the cumin, salt, garlic and oregano and cook over medium high heat, stirring frequently, until the onions begin to brown (5 minutes more).
6. Stir in 1 cup of the bean cooking liquid (or water, which can cause less flatulence) and heat to nearly a boil. Feel free to start with a half cup and see how thin it gets, then add more only if you need it.

7. Blend or mash the beans and cooking liquid:
    - *To use an immersion blender:* Add the beans, stir until everything is heated (it will be quick if you just cooked the beans!) and then remove from heat to blend with the tool.
    - *To use a potato masher:* Add half the beans. Use the potato masher to mash them. Add the rest of the beans and mash more.
8. You can leave the mixture uneven with some whole beans or mash until fairly smooth.
9. Stir well and make sure the beans are thoroughly heated over low heat (they'll stick to the bottom badly if the heat gets too high or you forget to stir).
10. When most of the water has been absorbed, turn off the heat.
11. Stir in cheese, if using.

Notes

- Makes about 4 - 5 cups or 2+ cans worth.

Simple Cheese Sauce

MAKES 1+ CUP *ADVANCED 8*

Ingredients

- 2 Tbs. (two tablespoons) butter *30 mL*
- 2 Tbs. (two tablespoons) white or whole wheat flour *30 mL*
  (GF option: Use buckwheat flour)
- 1 c. (one cup) whole milk *240 mL*
- 3/4 c. (three-fourths cup) shredded cheese *90 grams*
  [Sharp cheddar is yummy, use part Romano or Parmesan for an edge]

Optional add-ins

- 1/4 tsp. (one-fourth teaspoon) salt *1.2 mL*
- 1/8 tsp. (one-eighth teaspoon) black pepper *.6 mL*
- 1/4 - 1/2 tsp. (one-fourth to one-half teaspoon) garlic powder
  1.2 - 2.5 mL

Instructions

1. In a medium pot, melt the butter over medium-low heat. If it starts bubbling and popping a lot, turn the heat down.
2. When the butter is totally liquid, add the flour. Stir it together to form a paste. *(This is a roux, pronounced "roo" like the little kangaroo in Winnie the Pooh.)*
3. Over medium or medium-low heat, watch for the paste to bubble.
4. Once it is bubbling, stir it around for about a minute. You can set a timer or count to 60 while stirring.
5. Carefully pour the cup of milk into the pot. You can turn the heat up to high if you want.
6. Stir every so often, scraping the bottom of the pot well so the milk doesn't stick to the pot.
7. Once you see some bubbling, turn the heat down to medium or lower.

8. Stir the whole time until it all thickens up. (This is a bechamel, a fancy French word for a white sauce, pronounced "besh-uh-mel.")
9. Turn the heat to low. Add the shredded cheese and stir to melt it all into the sauce.
10. Yum! Serve warm.

Notes

- You can experiment with adding garlic powder, salt, and pepper for a little extra flavor. If you used white cheese and you want your sauce to look yellow, sprinkle in some dried turmeric — which is what makes mustard yellow, but it won't taste like mustard.

- Serve with steamed vegetables, over potatoes, on pasta or rice, with chips and salsa...any way you can think of, because everything is better with cheese! ;)

Simple Grain-Free Cheese Sauce

MAKES 1+ CUP *ADVANCED 8*

Ingredients

- 2 Tbs. (two tablespoons) butter, *optional* *30 mL*
- 1 Tbs. (one tablespoon) arrowroot powder *15 mL*
- 1 c. (one cup) whole milk *240 mL*
- 3/4 c. (three-fourths cup) shredded cheese *90 grams*
  [Sharp cheddar is yummy, use part Romano or Parmesan for an edge]

Optional add-ins

- 1/4 tsp. (one-fourth teaspoon) salt *1.2 mL*
- 1/8 tsp. (one-eighth teaspoon) black pepper *.6 mL*
- 1/4 - 1/2 tsp. (one-fourth to one-half teaspoon) garlic powder *1.2 - 2.5 mL*

Instructions

1. In a medium pot, melt the butter (if using) over medium-low heat. If it starts bubbling and popping a lot, turn the heat down.
2. Pour about 3/4 of the milk into the pot and heat over medium. Stir so it doesn't scald (stick to the bottom).
3. In a jar with a tightly fitting lid, pour the remaining milk and the arrowroot powder.
4. Put the lid on tightly and shake until everything is mixed up completely.
5. Once the milk in the pot is bubbling, carefully pour the milk/starch mixture into the pot.
6. Cook over medium heat until it begins to bubble. Stir and scrape the whole bottom every so often so the milk doesn't burn and stick to the pot. (You can put the lid on the pot to heat it faster, but if the milk bubbles when you're not looking, it might boil over and make a mess. Watch closely!)
7. When you see bubbles, turn the heat down to low or medium-low — whatever keeps some bubbles happening —

and stir constantly until it begins to thicken up. *(This is a grain-free bechamel, a fancy French word for a white sauce, pronounced "besh-uh-mel.")*

8. Turn the heat to low. Add the shredded cheese and stir to melt it all into the sauce.
9. Yum! Serve warm.

Notes

- If you feel like your sauce should be thicker, don't just add more arrowroot powder to the sauce! It will get all lumpy. You'll have to shake another tablespoon of starch in your jar with 1/4 cup more milk and mix that into your pot. And remember: your sauce WILL get a lot thicker as it cools down and also after adding the cheese.

- You can experiment with adding garlic powder, salt, and pepper for a little extra flavor. If you used white cheese and you want your sauce to look yellow, sprinkle in some dried turmeric — which is what makes mustard yellow, but it won't taste like mustard.

- Serve with steamed vegetables, over potatoes, on pasta or rice, with chips and salsa...any way you can think of, because everything is better with cheese! ;)

Simple Chicken Rice Soup

SERVES 4 *ADVANCED 1*

Ingredients

- 3 carrots
- 3 celery ribs
- 4 - 6 c. (four to six cups) homemade chicken stock *960 mL - 1.4 litres*
- 1/2 c. (one-half cup) uncooked white or brown rice *95 grams*
- 2 c. (two cups) cooked chicken *250 grams*
- 1/2 - 1 tsp. (one-half to one teaspoon) dried thyme *2.5 - 5 mL*
- 1 tsp. (one teaspoon) salt *5 mL*
- 1/4 tsp. (one-fourth teaspoon) pepper, *optional* *1.2 mL*

Instructions

1. Cut the carrots into half-moon slices.
2. Dice the celery or slice into half-moons.
3. In a large pot, combine all the ingredients.
4. Bring to a boil over high heat with the cover on.
5. Turn the heat to low and set a timer for 15 minutes for white rice, 45 minutes for brown rice.
6. When the timer goes off, check the rice to see if it's soft. It's likely it will need more time. Add 10 minutes and check again.
7. Taste test to see if you need any more salt or seasoning.
8. (If it's not thick enough, use up to a full cup of rice next time. You can also use leftover cooked rice.)

Notes

- Visit *www.KidsCookRealFood.com/recipes* to learn how to make homemade chicken stock or how to roast a whole chicken. You can get the cooked chicken for this recipe with these processes.

Simple Salad Ideas

BEGINNER 7

List of Greens

lettuce (romaine, boston bib, red lettuce, etc.)
spinach
salad greens mix
cabbage (shredded coleslaw style)
baby kale

List of Vegetables

carrots
peas (fresh, frozen, or thawed)
sugar snap pea pods
peppers (green or colored)
tomatoes (cherry, roma, heirloom, etc.)
cucumbers
broccoli
red onion
cauliflower
green onion
radishes
corn
beets (roasted or pickled)
avocado
mushrooms

List of Special Extras

nuts (pecans, walnuts, slivered almonds)
seeds (pepitas, sunflower, etc.)
dried fruit (cranberries, apples, figs, etc.)
fresh fruit (apples, pears, grapes, clementines, strawberries, blueberries, etc.)
mandarin oranges
cheese (cheddar, mozzarella, goat, feta, blue cheese)
hard boiled egg
croutons (ideally homemade)
cooked beans
sun dried tomatoes
olives
cooked meats (chicken, turkey, bacon, ham, roast beef, etc.)

Veggie Stir Fry

BEGINNER 3, ADVANCED 3

Instructions

1. Get a large pan hot and "sizzle test" it.
2. Add 2 tablespoons *(30 mL)* of oil.
3. Add onions and peppers.
4. Add other vegetables, according to the Slow To Fast Vegetable Timing Chart.
5. Stir the vegetables around, scraping the bottom. Move food from the bottom to top and inside to out.

Slow to Fast Vegetable Timing Chart

Vegetables may take longer or shorter times depending on how high your heat is and whether you have a lid on or not. But relative to one another, they stay pretty standardized. Here's the order you should add vegetables to your pot in a mixed-veggie sauté (assuming they are sliced thinly; chunks will always take longer). For the complete chart, along with helpful information, see the Advanced Class 5 section of Kids Cook Real Food: Cooking Class Curriculum.

1. Onions	**10. Brussels Sprouts**
2. Peppers	**11. Cabbage**
3. Raw Potatoes	**12. Woody Bok Choy/Swiss Chard Ribs**
4. Mushrooms	**13. Broccoli Florets**
5. Thinly Sliced Carrots	**14. Asparagus**
6. Celery	**15. Green Beans**
7. Cauliflower	**16. Peas**
8. Water Chestnuts	**17. Radishes**
9. Leeks	**18. Eggplant**

Whole Wheat (Soaked) Tortillas

MAKES 10-12 *INTERMEDIATE 7*

Ingredients

- 2 c. (two cups) white whole wheat flour *240 grams*
- 1 tsp. (one teaspoon) salt *5 mL*
- 1/4 c. (one-fourth cup) solid fat: palm shortening, lard, or coconut oil *25 grams*
- 1/2 c. (one-half cup) liquid, any combination of water and whey *120 mL*

Instructions

The flour in this tortilla dough can be "soaked" to improve digestibility, or step 6 can be skipped and they can be made all in one go. Visit www.KidsCookRealFood.com/recipes for more info about soaking grains for digestibility.

1. Measure the flour into a medium-sized bowl. (If not soaking, mix salt in now.)
2. Use a pastry blender to cut in the solid fat.
3. Use a fork to mix in the whey and water. They whey can be skipped if you're not soaking the dough.
4. Keep mixing and make sure all the flour is part of the wet dough. If it's not, add more water (1 tablespoon *(15 mL)* at a time) until all the flour gets mixed in. You may need up to 4 tablespoons *(60 mL)*.
5. Knead the dough about 5 minutes until it looks even and you can see air bubbles.
6. Cover and allow to rest overnight in the bowl on the counter. (This is the "soak.")
7. The next day, add the salt and knead for 5 minutes until the salt is completely mixed in. Divide the dough into 8 - 11 balls.
8. Sprinkle some flour on a flat surface, like a cutting board.
9. Roll each ball flat as thinly as possible. Use more flour if the dough sticks to your rolling pin.

10. Heat an ungreased electric griddle to 400° F *(200° C)* or a cast iron skillet over medium-high heat.
11. Fry the tortillas about 20-40 seconds, until you can see brown spots on the bottom when you peek.
12. Flip the tortilla and fry the other side until there are brown flecks too. The second side sometimes cooks faster.
13. Remove to a plate. Serve warm or refrigerate.

Recipe Index

If you liked these recipes, be sure to check out the complete collection of recipe eBooks by Katie Kimball!
Go to *www.KitchenStewardship.com/ebooks* for access.

Healthy Snacks to Go
Over 45 recipes to get you on your way with real food, real fast
Fast food doesn't mean processed food. The 2nd edition includes more recipes, more bonuses and covers nearly every food allergy out there – all without a pre-packaged food. Finally, a book filled with truly healthy snacks!

Better Than a Box
How to Transform Your Processed Foods Recipes into Whole Foods Favorites
20 recipe reverse engineering demonstrations, 35 remake resources and 25 ready-to-cook recipes make cooking family-favorite recipes using whole foods a whole lot easier. Get rid of the processed foods and make dinner better than a box!

The Healthy Breakfast Book
Cereal-free Secrets to Starting the Day with Real Food
With over 50 family-friendly recipes, key tips for planning ahead, hosting a brunch and the one food to have on hand to kickstart your family's "5-a-day" fruits and veggies at breakfast, this book will be your guide to healthier mornings.

The Healthy Lunch Box
Sandwich-free Secrets to Packing a Real Food Lunch
45 recipes, 100+ resources and loaded with strategies to streamline your packing process, stock your pantry with emergency backups for your backups, and send healthy, delicious food in the lunch box, no matter how old your eater is – and there's not a sandwich in sight.

The Family Camping Handbook
Real Food in the Big Woods
You don't have to compromise with pre-packaged meals and processed foods just because you're cooking over a campfire. 36 recipes and a Paleo/Primal/Grain-free adaptation guide are at your disposal to make your next frugal vacation a success.

The Everything Beans Book
30 Frugal, Nutrient-Packed Recipes for Every Eater
From nutrition and storage to preparation and kid (and adult) friendly recipes, this book is the A to Z of beans. Beat the rising cost of food prices with thoroughly tested recipes that cover every meal, including dessert!

Smart Sweets
30 Desserts to Indulge your Sweet Tooth
Can dessert really have less sugar, soaked or sprouted whole grains, probiotics, or even vegetables and still taste good? Absolutely! Whip up a batch of healthified cookies, bars, brownies, cakes, pies and more, and win over even the sweetest tooth!

Made in United States
Orlando, FL
03 January 2025